TWO TRUTHS AND A MYTH

THE Apollo 11 MOON LANDING

SPOT THE MYTHS

by Matt Chandler

Published by Capstone Press, an imprint of Capstone
1710 Roe Crest Drive, North Mankato, Minnesota 56003
capstonepub.com

Library of Congress Cataloging-in-Publication Data
Names: Chandler, Matt, author.
Title: The Apollo 11 moon landing : spot the myths / by Matt Chandler.
Description: North Mankato, Minnesota : Capstone Press, [2024] | Series:
Two truths and a myth | Includes bibliographical references and index.
Audience: Ages 8-11 | Audience: Grades 4-6 | Summary: "In July 1969,
astronauts on the Apollo 11 spacecraft became the first people to land
on the moon. Since then, people have told stories about the historic
event. Did an unmanned Soviet spacecraft crash into the moon while the
Apollo astronauts were on it? Did Neil Armstrong know what he was going
to say before he stepped onto the moon's surface? Read the stories. Then
see if you can spot the myths!"— Provided by publisher.
Identifiers: LCCN 2023031084 (print) | LCCN 2023031085 (ebook) | ISBN 9781669062578
(hardcover) | ISBN 9781669062806 (paperback) | ISBN
9781669062608 (pdf) | ISBN 9781669062813 (epub) | ISBN 9781669062820
(kindle edition)
Subjects: LCSH: Apollo 11 (Spacecraft)—Juvenile literature. | Space flight
to the moon—Juvenile literature.
Classification: LCC TL789.8.U6A5 C43 2024 (print) | LCC TL789.8.U6A5
(ebook) | DDC 629.45/4—dc23/eng/20230809
LC record available at https://lccn.loc.gov/2023031084
LC ebook record available at https://lccn.loc.gov/2023031085

Editorial Credits
Editor: Carrie Sheely; Designer: Bobbie Nuytten; Media Researcher: Rebekah Hubstenberger;
Production Specialist: Whitney Schaefer

Source Notes
Page 4, "The Eagle has landed, " Kiner, Deb, "'The Eagle has landed': Armstrong, Aldrin become
the first men to walk on the moon," Penn Live, July 20, 2021, https://www.pennlive.com/nation-
world/2021/07/the-eagle-has-landed-armstrong-aldrin-become-the-first-men-to-walk-on-the-
moon.html Accessed January 26, 2023.
Page 7, "That's one small step . . . " "July 20, 1969: One Giant Leap For Mankind," NASA, July 20,
2019, https://www.nasa.gov/mission_pages/apollo/apollo11.html Accessed January 26, 2023.
Page 8, "That's all fiction," "The 11 Biggest Myths About Neil Armstrong, First Man on the
Moon," CBS News, July 18, 2014, https://www.cbsnews.com/media/the-11-biggest-myths-about-
neil-armstrong-first-man-on-the-moon/ Accessed January 26, 2023.
Page 8, "They never happened," James R. Hansen. First Man: The Life of Neil A. Armstrong. New
York: Simon & Schuster, 2018.
Page 12, "I didn't really . . . " "Apollo 11: The Fight for the First Footprint on the Moon," The
Guardian, May 25, 2019, https://www.theguardian.com/science/2019/may/25/apollo-11-the-
fight-over-the-first-footprint-neil-armstrong-buzz-aldrin-nasa-1969 Accessed January 26, 2023.

Printed and bound in the USA. PO 5626

TABLE OF CONTENTS

Words in **bold** are in the glossary.

"The Eagle has landed." American astronaut Neil Armstrong spoke those famous words on July 20, 1969. Armstrong and Edwin "Buzz" Aldrin had just landed on the surface of the moon. They were joined by astronaut Michael Collins. He remained in **orbit** around the moon. The historic event marked the first time people had landed on the moon. About 600 million people watched the Apollo 11 mission on live television.

Since 1969, people have been fascinated by the moon landing. Countless books, movies, and television programs have been made about the event. All that talk has led to many myths.

You are here to be a detective. Three statements will be presented together. One of them is a myth or **misconception**. Can you spot the myths hidden among the facts?

People in Milan, Italy, watch the Apollo 11 moon landing.

HOW CAN I TELL WHAT'S TRUTH AND WHAT'S A MYTH?

START HERE. ⇨ Does the statement include words like "all" or "none"?

YES ⇨ It might be a myth. Words such as "all" or "none" often simplify complicated topics. These statements might not be true.

NO ⇨ Does the statement include specific information, such as names or dates?

YES ⇨ It might be true. Details are important when dealing with facts. The more details a statement provides, the more likely it is to be true.

NO ⇨ It might be a myth. Vague facts without detail might be made up. It's good to question statements that don't include specific details.

Neil Armstrong

TRUTH OR MYTH?

1. BEFORE HE WAS AN ASTRONAUT, NEIL ARMSTRONG WAS A FIGHTER PILOT IN THE UNITED STATES NAVY.

Armstrong flew 78 combat missions during the Korean War (1950-1953). He was awarded two Gold Stars for his heroics in the war. Armstrong said he believed flying in combat was more dangerous than walking on the moon.

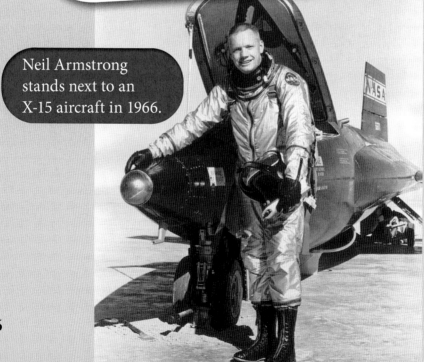

Neil Armstrong stands next to an X-15 aircraft in 1966.

2. ARMSTRONG DID NOT KNOW WHAT HE WAS GOING TO SAY WHEN HE STOOD ON THE MOON UNTIL THE MEN HAD LANDED.

As he stepped from the landing **module**, Armstrong spoke his famous quote, "That's one small step for a man, one giant leap for mankind." He didn't have it planned before then.

3. WHEN HE WAS A YOUNG BOY, ARMSTRONG TOLD FRIENDS AND FAMILY THAT HE WOULD FLY TO THE MOON SOMEDAY.

Armstrong became famous after the moon landing. People who knew him throughout his life gave interviews about him. One of the most famous stories said that when he was a boy, Armstrong predicted he would fly to the moon.

THE MYTH

WHEN HE WAS A YOUNG BOY, ARMSTRONG TOLD FRIENDS AND FAMILY THAT HE WOULD FLY TO THE MOON SOMEDAY.

The tales told about Armstrong dreaming he would grow up to be an astronaut are not true. The myth began in 1969. One of his former teachers gave interviews claiming Armstrong told him he dreamed of flying to the moon. When asked about it years later, Armstrong said simply, "That's all fiction."

The myth was boosted by **amateur** astronomer Jacob Zint. He too gave interviews and claimed a young Armstrong talked to him about what it would be like on the moon. Once again, when asked about these stories, Armstrong said, "They never happened."

Neil Armstrong during an interview in 1969

One reason this myth lasted so long was because of Armstrong himself. He did not like to do many interviews. People told their made-up stories for years before he finally corrected them.

1. AN IMPORTANT PART BROKE DURING THE MISSION. ALDRIN USED A PEN TO FIX IT.

When getting back into the lunar module, Aldrin's backpack banged into a switch. Without the switch, the engine would not fire. The astronauts would be trapped on the moon. Aldrin used a felt-tip pen he had in his pocket to repair the part and start the engine.

2. ALDRIN DID NOT TAKE ANY PHOTOS OF NEIL ARMSTRONG'S HISTORIC FIRST STEPS ONTO THE MOON'S SURFACE.

All the photos of an astronaut looking at the camera are Aldrin. The only photo of Armstrong is a distant photo of the landscape with him near the module.

3. ALDRIN WAS ANGRY BECAUSE HE DID NOT GET TO BE THE FIRST PERSON TO WALK ON THE MOON.

Aldrin is famous. But Armstrong is more famous. Only one person in history got to be the first person to set foot on the surface of the moon. NASA chose Armstrong, upsetting Aldrin.

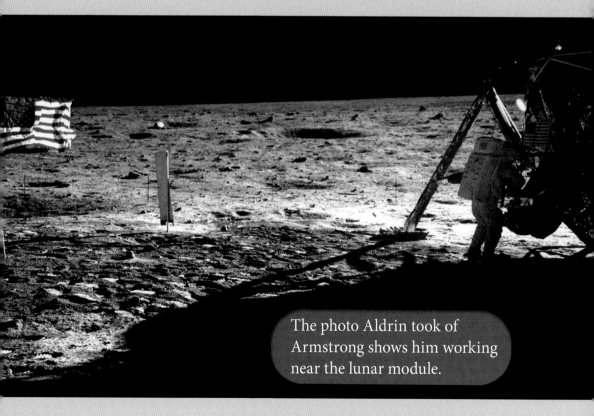

The photo Aldrin took of Armstrong shows him working near the lunar module.

THE MYTH

ALDRIN WAS ANGRY BECAUSE HE DID NOT GET TO BE THE FIRST PERSON TO WALK ON THE MOON.

The myth developed because many people assumed Aldrin would be mad because he missed out on this historic moment. Other astronauts even said he was angry. Some people believed that is why he didn't take any photos of Armstrong on the moon. It was his way of getting back at him because he was upset.

Aldrin has always insisted he was not mad that Armstrong was chosen to go first. "I didn't really want to be the first person to step on the moon. I knew the media would never let that person alone," he said later in life.

The real reason there are no photos of Armstrong's first steps is because Armstrong wore the specially designed space camera. It was secured to the chest of his spacesuit. When Aldrin did have the camera, both men said they were focused on other things. They had a lot of work to do. Taking extra photos wasn't on their checklist.

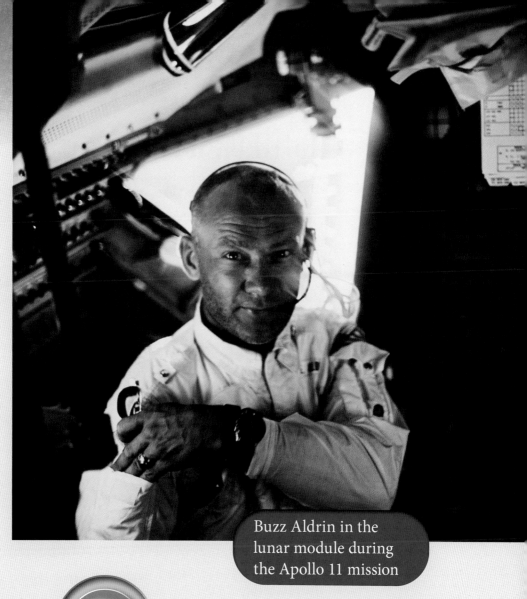

Buzz Aldrin in the lunar module during the Apollo 11 mission

FACT

Neil Armstrong left the first footprints on the moon, but neither astronaut photographed them. Instead, the famous photo of the footprint on the moon is one left by Aldrin.

Left Behind on the Moon

TRUTH OR MYTH?

1. THE FOOTPRINTS ARMSTRONG AND ALDRIN LEFT ON THE MOON ARE STILL THERE.

Because there is no wind on the moon's surface, the original footprints did not get blown away. There is also no rain to wash away the footprints.

2. AN UNMANNED SOVIET SPACECRAFT CRASHED INTO THE MOON DURING THE AMERICAN MISSION.

The spacecraft had been circling the moon for several days. It crashed into the surface on July 21, 1969. Aldrin and Armstrong were more than 300 miles (480 kilometers) away, so they did not see the crash. The wreckage is still on the moon today.

3. THE AMERICAN FLAG THAT THE MEN PLANTED ON THE MOON'S SURFACE WAS BLOWING IN THE WIND. THIS PROVED THE MOON LANDING WAS FAKED.

Because there is no wind on the moon, a flag could not flow outward. But the flag on the moon was flowing away from the pole. This proved the landing was really filmed on Earth.

The Soviet unmanned spacecraft Luna 10 was the first to enter the moon's orbit in 1966.

THE MYTH

THE AMERICAN FLAG THAT THE MEN PLANTED ON THE MOON'S SURFACE WAS BLOWING IN THE WIND. THIS PROVED THE MOON LANDING WAS FAKED.

After the mission, some people said the moon landing was faked. They said the blowing flag helped prove their claim. But NASA had added a bar across the top to hold the flag out so it would look better on television and in pictures. When the astronauts tried to extend the bar at the top, it got stuck. This led to the appearance that the flag was blowing in the wind. But it was an **illusion**.

The myth was supported in a video of Aldrin planting the flag on the moon. In the film, the flag can be seen "waving." Aldrin later explained that as he wiggled the pole to get it deeper into the moon dirt, it made it look like it was waving. In the video, the flag never moves once it is planted.

Armstrong (left) and Aldrin (right) stand by the U.S. flag on the moon.

FACT

The flag the Apollo 11 astronauts planted on the moon is one of the most famous American flags in history. NASA purchased the flag for $5.50.

Exploring the Moon

TRUTH OR MYTH?

1. THE ASTRONAUTS BROUGHT BACK MORE THAN 45 POUNDS (20 KILOGRAMS) OF ROCKS AND DUST FROM THE MOON TO STUDY.

After the Apollo 11 mission, scientists were able to study materials from another space body for the first time. They wanted to do the studies to find out if there was life in space.

2. THE ASTRONAUTS REPORTED THAT THE DUST ON THE MOON SMELLED LIKE A MIX OF WET ASHES AND EXPLODED GUNPOWDER.

Aldrin and Armstrong were the first humans to get a sense of how moon dust smelled. Humans were fascinated to learn every detail from the only people to ever step onto the moon's surface. That included what it smelled like.

3. THERE IS NO GRAVITY ON THE MOON.

NASA developed special training for the astronauts to help them adjust to being without gravity. In one example, they hung Armstrong and Aldrin sideways and made them walk along walls.

A moon rock

THE MYTH

THERE IS NO GRAVITY ON THE MOON.

The myth that there was no gravity on the moon was born from the fact that no one had ever been there. Movies and stories told of "floating in space," so many people believed the moon had no gravity. The gravity on the moon is roughly 1/6 as strong as Earth's.

Aldrin was the first person to prove the gravity myth was false. He conducted tests to judge the impact less gravity had on a person's ability to walk, turn, and even bounce. They showed the moon's softer gravitational pull. If there were truly zero gravity, Aldrin would have floated away!

Aldrin in training under conditions of weightlessness

Return to Earth

1. THE ASTRONAUTS HAD TO LIVE IN ISOLATION BEFORE THE MISSION AND FOR 21 DAYS WHEN THEY RETURNED TO EARTH.

NASA built the Lunar Receiving Laboratory in Houston, Texas. It allowed the astronauts to be in **quarantine**. Scientists were worried the men might bring back poisons or **organisms** that could be harmful.

2. THE THREE ASTRONAUTS WHO COMPLETED THE APOLLO 11 MISSION NEVER RETURNED TO SPACE.

NASA carried out five more manned flights to the moon. Despite their experience, NASA never chose any of the Apollo 11 astronauts to participate in any of them.

3. BUZZ ALDRIN SAID THE MOON LANDING WAS FAKED.

Many **conspiracy theories** exist about the Apollo 11 flight being fake. Most were proven false. Then an interview was released of Aldrin. In it, he talked about how NASA had used video **animation** to show the world the moon landing.

An astronaut stands on the moon near a Lunar Roving Vehicle in 1972.

THE MYTH

BUZZ ALDRIN SAID THE MOON LANDING WAS FAKED.

Aldrin has never said the moon landing was faked or staged. This myth came from a 2000 television interview he gave. In it, he said people who watched the moon landing on television were watching animation. NASA did use animation to show television viewers what the moon landing would look like. That is because there were no cameras on the moon to film the craft arriving. Once the hatch was opened, the true footage began. Still, people created the myth that the entire mission was animated footage.

Aldrin participates in interviews in 2009.

People who believe in conspiracies work hard to prove them. This led to another example of trying to "prove" Aldrin said the moon landing was faked. Someone took parts of three different interviews Aldrin gave over many years. They took parts of sentences from each and blended them together into one clip. It made it look like Aldrin said the landing was faked. It was the video that was fake.

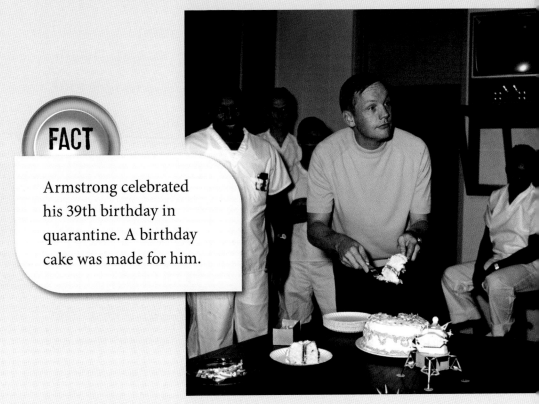

FACT

Armstrong celebrated his 39th birthday in quarantine. A birthday cake was made for him.

Life After Apollo 11

TRUTH OR MYTH?

1. THE FLAG ALDRIN AND ARMSTRONG PLANTED IS NO LONGER STANDING. SCIENTISTS THINK THE FLAG COULD HAVE BROKEN DOWN COMPLETELY.

As the astronauts left the moon, they saw the flag get knocked over. The moon gets struck by more than 33,000 **asteroids** each year. It has cycles of very hot and very cold temperatures. **Radiation** from sunlight is intense on the moon. Scientists think the harsh conditions could have caused the flag to fade and break down. There may be nothing left of it.

2. ALDRIN SAID HE SAW AN UNIDENTIFIED FLYING OBJECT (UFO) WHILE ON THE MISSION.

After returning, Aldrin claimed to have seen a UFO on the way to the moon. In 2018, the *Daily Star* said that Aldrin passed a lie detector test. It confirmed what Aldrin said.

3. AFTER ARMSTRONG QUIT NASA, HE BECAME A TEACHER AND LIVED ON A FARM.

Armstrong never wanted to be famous. Once he returned to Earth, Armstrong walked away from NASA for a simple life. He worked as a professor from 1971 to 1979. He lived on a farm in Ohio.

An asteroid flies toward the moon.

THE MYTH

ALDRIN SAID HE SAW AN UNIDENTIFIED FLYING OBJECT (UFO) WHILE ON THE MISSION.

Aldrin has repeatedly denied the claim that he saw a UFO. Still, the newspaper presented what it said was proof. But it was all false. They had never interviewed Aldrin for the test. They just used audio clips of former interviews.

Aldrin had given an interview where he talked about seeing a strange light following their ship in space. But he never took a lie detector test. He also said he did not believe it was an alien ship. Even though it has been proven false, the internet has kept the UFO myth alive.

The Apollo 11 moon landing has fascinated people for more than 50 years. It has also led to many myths. How many myths did you spot?

Neil Armstrong, Michael Collins, Buzz Aldrin (from left to right), 1969

GLOSSARY

amateur (AM-uh-chur)—done for fun instead of for money

animation (a-nuh-MAY-shuhn)—a design made to make something look like real movement

asteroid (AS-tuh-roid)—a large space rock that moves around the sun; asteroids are too small to be called planets

conspiracy theory (kun-SPIR-uh-see THEE-uh-ree)—an idea that explains an event as a result of a secret plot

illusion (i-LOO-zhuhn)—something that appears to be real but isn't

misconception (mis-kuhn-SEP-shuhn)—a wrong or inaccurate idea

module (MAH-jul)—a part of the total structure of a space vehicle

orbit (OR-bit)—the path an object follows while circling an object in space

organism (OR-guh-niz-uhm)—a living thing

quarantine (KWOR-uhn-teen)—the act of keeping something separate from a larger group

radiation (ray-dee-AY-shuhn)—the sending out of energy rays

READ MORE

Gauthier, Kelly. *Discovering the Moon*. Kennebunkport, ME: Applesauce Press, 2019.

Halls, Kelly Milner. *Apollo 11 Q&A*. Emeryville, CA: Rockridge Press, 2021.

Maranville, Amy. *The Apollo 11 Moon Landing: A Day That Changed America*. North Mankato, MN: Capstone, 2022.

INTERNET SITES

NASA: Apollo 11
nasa.gov/mission_pages/apollo/apollo-11.html

National Air and Space Museum: Apollo Program
airandspace.si.edu/explore/topics/space/apollo-program

National Geographic Kids: The Moon Landing
kids.nationalgeographic.com/history/article/moon-landing

INDEX

ABOUT THE AUTHOR

Matt Chandler is the author of more than 80 books for children and thousands of articles published in newspapers and magazines. He writes mostly nonfiction books with a focus on sports, ghosts and haunted places, and graphic novels. Matt lives in New York.

Image Credits
Alamy: The NASA Library, 17, 25; Associated Press: 4; Getty Images: All About Space Magazine, 15, Hulton Archive, 6, Mark Wilson, 24, Ronald Dumont/Express, 9, Space Frontiers, 13; NASA: 11, 19, JSC, Cover, 20, 21, Marshall Space Flight Center, 23, 29; Shutterstock: Apostrophe, design element (texture), icon99, design element (footprint), LineTale, design element (space icons), Marti Bug Catcher, 27